SOMETHING
OF
VALUE

Poetic Thoughts
of
An Average Christian Guy

(And Five Short Stories)

RAWLAND STORM

WESTBOW°
PRESS
A DIVISION OF THOMAS NELSON
& ZONDERVAN

WestBow Press books may be ordered through booksellers or by contacting:

WestBow Press
A Division of Thomas Nelson & Zondervan
1663 Liberty Drive
Bloomington, IN 47403
www.westbowpress.com
1 (866) 928-1240

ISBN: 978-1-4908-3543-3 (sc)
ISBN: 978-1-4908-3544-0 (e)

Library of Congress Control Number: 2014907665

Printed in the United States of America.

WestBow Press rev. date: 05/20/2014

Contents

Stories

A Way in the Manger

One star shone in the doorway;
Another lay inside;
The first, created;
The second, born;
Yet, destined to collide
Gently in a manger—
Their journeys took so long—
Each piece in a puzzle placed
Exactly where each one belonged;
One star shone in a doorway;
Another lay inside;
Both still shine
On your life and mine;
Yet, some still choose to hide...
From the one who made them;
From the one, which lights their way;
They still look in from the doorway...
Will you leave, or will you stay?

You were, after-all, all invited in.

All There Is

All there is
to life
is
take life
as it comes;

Admit
you can't always
change it
But
sometimes
you can...

If you know
the difference
you will be
impressed
by the world
around you
and seldom
get depressed...

But
if you do,
Remember
you
are not in this thing
Alone—
God
wouldn't do that
to you;
It's something
He
does not condone...
It's also why
He made a woman

Besides
making a man...
They were made
For each other...
As only The God can...

Just
look around
and
you will see
there's
more to life
Than you...
But
somehow
each thing
in this world
is special—
Each
has a job
to do...

And
so do you—
You have a
Purpose—
You
just have to find
your place...
And
really
that is
All There Is
to Life—
To meet it
Face to Face.

Angel's Evening Song

As angels sang of a miracle—
God's Son, as a human born;
Shepherds gazed, beyond amazed;
This early Christmas morn;

First, they were frightened;
Then enlightened
To hear of God's promise kept;
So they ran with haste—
No time to waste;
To get to where the Savior slept;

The angels' evening song was continued
As shepherd sang, with joy, each word;
At first their voices raised;
But soon they silently praised
This Jesus Christ, their Lord;

The angels' words were repeated
By shepherds to everyone they met;
And those who heard the shepherd's story
Retold it to spread God's glory;
And it's not stopped being retold, yet.

Are You The Answer to Your Prayers

There have been so many times
I have prayed
For the answers to some pain;
Physical, spiritual,
Financial loss, weight gain;

There have been so many prayers
Directed up above,
When all I needed was
More self-control or motivation—
Not help, or charity, or even
God's love.

I pray for someone to help others—
Feed them, clothe them,
Or get them a job;
But I have food galore
And clothes? I have more
Than kernels on a big corn cob;

Why do I bother
The God who gave me
Everything I need,
With prayers for others
To do what I do not—
Am I afraid I will not succeed?

Or am I too busy, selfish, proud
To provide the things
Which can give others wings—
To fly even with the crowd?

The next time
You feel the need
To pray for others
Think first,
"What is it I can do?
Did God give me
All that I need
So I can keep
It away from you?"

Or anyone else who
Really is now praying
For someone like me
And you
To see, hear, feel,
Sense, and know
We can make prayers
Come true.

Born to Die

Born to die—
As we all are...
But at least He had a choice...
Lived to try
To be perfect for us,
So we, too,
Would have a voice...
To ask
And receive
Forgiveness...
To ask and receive
Salvation;
Not just for one,
But every nation...
And the price?
Just believe.

Christmas is a Gift

Christmas
is a gift,
which
was exchanged—
for us—
at Easter.

Christmas Without Jesus

Christmas
Without Jesus
Is just another day
And night alone
In this big world
Without the star that shone
To guide us
To where the Savior lay
And so, we still are lost;
Searching
For the perfect gift...
Wond'ring what it will cost
And if payment can be made
By Mastercard, or Visa;
Or only cash or check;
Yet, the final toll
Is our soul
As, if now, we give-a-heck...
Still
The day will come
All too soon
When, in-full,
The debt, we must pay,
But we will find
There is no way
In the world
We can
Unless
We believe
That Saving began this day.

Do You Know What I Know? A Christmas Haiku

Snow falls silently;
A whispering wind still hears;
I look up...and see.

Don't Ever Think You're Not Beautiful

Beauty's not just on the outside;
Although you're beautiful to me.
No, it's not just on the surface;
It's not just what we see;
It's thoughts, and words, and actions;
It's kindness, caring, love;
It's who you are and what you are,
When seen from up above
The view that others usually take;
And that is from straight-on—
They just care about the outside—
They don't want to see beyond;
But I can see you're lonely;
I can see you cry...
You don't think you're good enough—
That is nothing, but a lie!
You're worth the world to God;
You're worth more than that to me;
You're good enough for anyone;
Except those who cannot see
The beauty that's inside
We don't let others see;
Unless they really want to look
For an eternity.

Forgive-Me-Nots

There is a flower in the garden
No one intends to grow...
It exists for no good reason;
Still, it is a flower we all sow...

I have seen them planted
And I have seen them bloom;
Yet, when they do, I try to ignore them;
For in my heart there is no room...

They are called, Forgive-Me-Nots;
They grow among the thorns;
They, too, produce painful pricks;
They, too, cause lives to be torn...

For when you walk down the path they line
You think nobody cares;
You think all your wrongs will last forever;
That everyone knows, and stares...

You feel you have no future;
Past mistakes, like these flowers, lie ahead;
You can't see beyond them;
So you pick them, although their air you dread...

It is then, when you are at your lowest—
After the weight of these flowers
You chose, has brought you down;
That God whispers in a still, small voice
To throw them all on the ground...

The second you do, your eyes are opened;
You see beyond these old, dead, Forgive-Me-Nots
To the most beautiful one God created
To replace it—
And named, Forget-Me-Not.

God's Frozen Tears

Are snowflakes
God's frozen tears of joy
For the birth of his Son?
And do they fall
So slowly
So that we can see each one?
And is each one different—
Just like each of us below?
And if we catch them
On our tongue,
During Christmas,
Do we all the answers know?

He Rose To The Occasion

He rose to the occasion—
He was the only One who could...
The path He took—perfect and straight;
His destination—a cross of wood;
He rose to the occasion—
Above death, and sin, and lies...
He rose to the occasion
So we, too, might also rise.

Heaven Watches Over Me

Heaven watches over me, until I realize
Love is but a word, until I see it in your eyes;
We both win, when we begin to know the Son will rise
In our hearts each day;

In our hearts each day
Is where Jesus does belong;
In our hearts each day
Our prayers become a song;

Heaven watches over us,
When love's no longer just a word
In our hearts each day.

How I'd Stop My Parent's Divorce

If I again was a child
And knew what I know now
I'd stop my parents' divorce
And this is how:

I'd ask Dad how he met Mom;
Was it love at first sight?
Did he plan to love her forever?
Or just overnight?

What did he notice first?
Was it her eyes?
Or maybe her smile?
Or that she was wise?

Was it her walk
And that wiggle, so slight
That stirred his imagination
And made her feel right?

Then I'd ask my Mom
The same questions—
To see if the answers
Were the same;
Okay, maybe not the one
About the wiggle—
He has a different frame!

Then I'd go back to my Dad;
Ask him when he knew
That it was love forever
And that it was true.

Was it their first kiss?
Or when they first held hands?
Was the answer found in their hearts?
Or in their glands?

Then back to Mom—
By now you see the routine—
I'd never ask them together—
That would be too mean...

Mom, is love forever?
Dad, how long does love last?
Mom, you said divorce was for never...
Dad, you said time was going too fast.

Dad, did you want kids?
Mom, do I have Daddy's dimple?
Dad, did you see me being born?
Mom, is child-birth simple?
Or, simply awful?
Or, simply great?
Or, simply worth it?
On a scale of 1-10, how do I rate?

Dad, have you ever been scared...
Especially at night?
Aren't you glad you, too, have Mom?
Does she also make your worries light?

Mom, remember the pictures you took?
What's your favorite one?
Dad likes the one of us at the zoo...
He says it was fun.

Dad, I'm glad I have you for a Dad...
Next to Mom, you're the Best!
Are you glad I'm a girl?
I'm glad, if you haven't already guessed.

Mom, I thank God you found Dad;
And for all you two do...
Someday I want to be just like you
And marry Daddy, too!

I love you BOTH.

I Always Think of You

When I look around this world
I always think of you;
When I see the flag unfurled
I see a dream come true;
When I go to bed I pray
You will give me one more day;
When I look around this world
I always think of you.

When the stars begin to shine
I always think of you;
When I realize they're mine
I see a dream come true;
When I go to bed I pray
You will give me one more day;
When the stars begin to shine
I always think of you.

When I see a newborn's eyes
I always think of you;
When I see the parents' eyes
I see a dream come true;
When I go to bed I pray
You will give me one more day;
When I see a newborn's eyes
I always think of you.

When the sun begins to set
I always think of you;
When I have not one regret
I see a dream come true;
When I go to bed I pray
You will give me one more day;
When the sun begins to set
I always think of you;

I Cannot Conceive

"I cannot conceive"
Is something
I often say,
When I think of life
And how we just
Throw it away...

The saddest words
of mice or men
are not the words,
"Might have been"...
The saddest words—
In fact, the most forlorn,
Are the words,
"I wish I were never born"...

And our response
Is, oh, so true:
"What would this world,
Or I, be without you?"

We never think, or say:
"Sorry, you are out of luck—
Your mother chose not to abort."
She legally could have done it,
But in your case
She chose your life ahead of her's;
Or even a court's...

But we could continue:
"Do you think
The thought of life without you
Ever crossed her mind...?

Once she imagined
You looking into her eyes
She could never find
Another who could
Make her life worth living...
Another who could
Give her the will to live
And share that life with you
And only want and need to give
You everything
She had and more...
Everything she never had...
But then she thought
Better of it...
Knowing if you
Are given everything
It is always bad..."

"And so she made you
Earn everything—
A kiss cost a smile...
A tear also deserved a kiss...
At first, you got confused
But you caught-on after awhile..."

"Sometimes there were hugs
And they eventually went both ways...
And truths were taught and often caught
By you watching her
And listening
To the words she'd say..."

"And now you say
You wish you were never born!"

"Maybe now your life
Might not seem that great,
But if you asked your mom or dad
You'd learn there is more to life than fate..."

"They gave their life to you—
From conception
Till today and beyond...
They may have gotten
Your life started,
But it is up to you
To continue on..."

"It might not
Always be easy...
In fact, it rarely is,
But it is Always life
And a life
Is something you should live...
If given the chance
Like you, thank God, have been...
You did not choose the time or place;
Or even the how or when..."

"But you now know the who—
What you now need to find out
Is the why...
If you were never born
The importance of life
Would be a lie..."

"And that
Is something
I cannot conceive."

I Never Had a Mother

I never had a mother
In the true sense of the word...
It's true I was conceived,
So I believed everything I heard:
That love would last forever—
After all
The result of it was me;
Who would not want to live forever?
I needed eternity...
To thank God for this life of mine—
I had so many plans—
I did not know it at the time
That life was sometimes
Out of my God's hands...

I never had a Father—
He never even knew
I was alive and growing
And that my eyes, like his,
Were blue—
He only wanted sex,
As if that was all it was—
Making love is more complex,
And that is because
Babies like me
Can be conceived;
Lives like mine
Are, believe me, a Fact...
Couples should not be deceived—
Sex is much more than just an act.

I never had parents—
People who really cared
About the unique me—
A life that wanted to be spared
From a prolonged death
And a shortened stay;
I never got to take a breath—
My choice was taken away.

I Never Was Aborted

I never was aborted...
Should I thank God
Or thank my Mom?
God got my life started,
But Mom provided me a home...
Safe within her body;
Then, safe within her arms...
And then Dad, too, followed through...
Protecting me from harm.

I never was aborted—
I thank God, and Mom, and Dad;
I'm glad they knew
I'd love life, too...
They made the best choice I never had.

I Remember You

I
Remember
Everything
Mom
Everyday
Mainly
Because
Everything
Reflects
Your
Omniscient
Understanding

I remember her because she never forgets/forgot me.

If Growing-Up Was Easy

If growing-up was easy
Anyone could do it...
So many try
Before they die
Yet, very few
Actually pursue it...

Growing-up
Sounded so exciting—
We had heard about it
Every day since birth—
So every day
We tried our best
To be the best on Earth...

Some grow-up
Quicker than others—
Some grow-up
Not at all...
Most of us
Are somewhere in between—
Somewhere along the way
We stall...

We find an age
We want to stay
So we decide
We will stop growing-up—
That we will always

Stay that way...
Then
As all others
Have discovered before us
This is easier said than done...
That there are so many things
We have to do—
We can't just do
The things that are fun...

And so we do
What is needed of us—
We do what life demands...
We find what
Worth living is—
If we can't
We put our life
Into God's hands...

And there we stay;
Whether we are
Pushed
Persuaded,
Or thrown...

All that I know
Is that one's life
Hasn't really been fulfilled
Until Up, they have grown.

Growing Up Is The Direction We Are Supposed To Grow.

If Only I Could Talk

In love I was conceived—
The Journey has begun
To be, perhaps, a daughter;
Or maybe a son;

The path is set, and yet,
I feel so insecure;
My feelings are intact,
Yet, my vision is a blur;

I've heard some people say
I'm not a person yet,
But who I will become
Is more sure than a sunset;

Generations from long ago
Combine in man and wife;
Parts of relatives from my past
In me, come back to life;

The color of my eyes—Granddad's;
My hair—my Mother's Mom;
And as for my love for life;
It's like that of an aunt of mine, long gone;

Why would someone stop
The accumulation of the past;
Put into just one cell...
Developing so fast?

My life is given me by God;
It's not even my own;
But if His will and mine is done
My soul will be born...
Complete with skin and bone.

If You Could Just See Me

If you could just see me forming inside
You'd witness a miracle some try to hide;
You'd see for yourself that I'm made just like you;
God's method is tried; God's method is true.

From conception, who I will become has been set;
There's naught you can do to change who you will get;
Unless, you of course, decide to stop my growth;
Only Mom can decide, not Dad—it doesn't take both.

I have just one chance to live—I won't come again;
'Til maybe in heaven we meet—only God can say when;
So please let me be born—there is so much to do;
God creates life for ALL—not just me and you.

I'm Worth a Lot to Jesus

I'm worth a lot to Jesus;
I'm worth so much He died;
Why He would do this for me
I still am mystified;
I feel so worthless sometimes
I just can't comprehend
How He loves me to the end.

When I am feeling lonely;
Depressed and, oh, so low;
My Savior holds His arms out;
A place for me to go;
Like rainbows after raindrops,
Or blue skies after snow;
His love covers me below.

We sometimes value ourselves
As others say we are;
But they can't see inside us;
They know us just so far;
We have a soul—God-given;
That only He can see;
And He loves us Constantly.

If I could have just one friend
To keep my whole life through;
My God would be that one friend;
His love is always true;
He made the whole world for me;
He's with me every day;
And I pray it stays that way.

I'm worth a lot to Jesus;
I'm worth so much He died;
Because He did this for me
I'll stay right by His side;
And there I will find others
Believing as I do...
Christian friends our whole life through.

I's of Wonder

I wonder why it takes so long
To know the truth from lies;

I wonder why I can't get past
The tears trapped in your eyes;

I wonder where it is that life starts...
Is it conception, birth, or love?

I wonder where life comes from...
Without, within, above?

I wonder why I wonder—
The truth's as clear as clear can be;

I wonder why I ignore the obvious
In exchange for living "free";

I wonder at the wonders
There are in this world to see;

And hear, touch, taste, and feel;
I wonder how they came to be;

I wonder why I believe
They're only meant for me?

Just One More Day With You

The suspense is killing me—
If I only had just one more day...
Perhaps this sense chilling me
Would somehow go away;

Just one more day, I'm begging you;
Though I cannot find a word;
I'm sure my thoughts are plaguing you;
Although, not one, you have heard;

There was a time I was all you thought of—
In your imagination I was first conceived;
Both hopes and dreams, there were a lot of...
If only, in us, you had believed;

I hope you pray...I know I will;
There's not much more that I can do;
Yet, you alone can my prayer fulfill...
Just one more day with you.

Written on behalf of every baby scheduled for an abortion.

Less Than Perfect is All Right

She had lost all sense of direction;
He had found the way;

She didn't know who she could talk to;
He knew of One, if only she would pray;

She only saw the darkness;
He, though, saw the stars;

She called him in desperation;
He drove to her in his car;

They once-upon-a-time had dated;
It was not a fairytale romance;

She had wanted more than he could give;
He wanted just the chance...

To prove there was more to life
Than more would give;
That less than perfect is all right;
For we all have a Savior—
The one born this very night...

They talked of hope;
They talked of peace;
They talked of right and wrong;

They talked of truth;
They talked of love;
They talked all night long;

In the morning, when the sun rose...
God's Son rose, also in her eyes;
And now she finally sees the light;
And the stars in God's sky.

Life As We Know It

Life
As we know it
Began,
Not as a twinkle in an eye;
Began,
Not as a tinkle
On a pregnancy test's supply;
Began,
Not when a Mother decides to keep it;
Not when some law says it's so;
Began
Not when an abortionist can no longer reap it—
To stop what we have all had the right to do—Grow;

It Begins
When we conceive it—
And not just in our mind;
It Begins
When, as we all deep-down believe it...
The same, exact way and moment
As your life did, and mine.

Making Love

When your Mother held you for the first time
After giving birth to you—
Looking deep into your eyes...
Confirming what she knew...
That next to your Father...
That next to God above
There was no one more important—
She was making love.

When your Father kissed you on the forehead
And promised he'd never leave you, or your Mom;
His touch silenced your first tears
And created lasting calm;
And by always being there—
Showing you what a father is made of;
He was not just doing his job—
He was making love.

When you finally grew-up
And had a family of your own;
Your actions showed you had not forgotten
The things you had always known—
That how you treat your spouse and children
Was learned from parents, now in Heaven above;
For their love for you lives on
As you continue making love.

Mom, For All You Ever Did

What can I say
That has never been said?
Well, if I don't try
I might as well be dead;
Or never born—
You never gave that a thought...
It's me you lived for—
You Gave—I Got...

You gave me your time—
Your most precious gift;
And when I was down
You gave me a lift...
To Heaven, if you could—
At least the stars above...
For all you ever did
Was reflect God's love...

A mere mirror you were—
I knew your every feeling;
In you I saw me,
But you were kneeling...
Praying to God
I would do well in school;
That I not break any laws;
That I follow the Rules;
That I have friends
I'd keep for life;
And that one day
I find a loving wife...

And when you slept
You dreamt for me;
And those dreams all came true—
If it wasn't for you
The me I am, I wouldn't be.

My Christmas Prayer For My Children

My Christmas prayer
Has always been
I see you in Heaven;
As I am sure
God, the Father's prayer
For His Son was, too,
When He was sent to Earth—
His life, for ours, to be given...

To be apart
For what I'm sure seemed like a lifetime—
Much more, no one, nor God, could take...
And so I pray this simple Christmas prayer;
Yet, it's the most important one
I will ever make.

Prayers are the least we can do
And the most we can do.

Open-Minded

Why be so open-minded,
When by doing so,
Your values fall right through...

When what you're told to accept
Is shallow,
But deep enough
To drown both me and you...

When Anything goes
Everything goes...away;
I've always known that to be true....

To accept the unacceptable
Is a very close-minded thing to do.

Perfection Insurrection

perceived
perfection
permeates
people's
perceptions
polluting
potential
possibilities.

As soon as we realize no one is perfect
We realize we are worth as much as anyone else...
Just ask God—He should know

Pitter-Patter

thoughts
cross my mind
like the pitter-patter
of a gently blowing rain...
like the pitter-patter
of an infant's first steps...
like the pitter-patter
of my first heartbeats
inside my Mother's womb...
giving meaning
to my life...
giving meaning
to the lives of others...
giving meaning
to each pitter-patter
I will ever see, hear, or feel.

Why is it that some sounds are noise, when you hear them,
but are remembered as music, when
they are no longer heard?

Psalm 1: To Watch Over Me

With you inside
I am not alone;
The day no longer
Just comes and goes,
But like the wind, flies;
And like the river, flows...

With your love
I am encircled
With no beginning
And no end...
Your love
Follows me around
As our
Two lives
Blend;

Your love is in the air—
It's in all I breathe, hear,
Smell, or feel;
Your love's the color
In the sky—
I can see it's real...

When you
Are outside
My reach
I watch you
Watch me—
It's true...

And we both see
The same forever:
You, loving me;
Me, loving you.

Separation From God

When the world was wise
We weren't worried...
We weren't worried at all...
With God in the skies
And in our lives
Each problem
Seemed too small
To cause concern
Or consternation
About the unknown
And the known;
For God made both;
Yet, still sent His Son
To die in our place
So we, too,
Might be His own...

Forever and eternally
So, really what was there to fear;
Except our own stupidity
About God not being near
To everything
We have in life...
To all we both love and hate;
So how can we
Call it wisdom
To separate
Church and state...

To separate
Science from Creation...
Evolution from Intelligent Design...
To separate God
From anything;
For nothing
Is really yours or mine...

When we say
Choice is more important
Than any unborn fetus

What do you think
God will say
When He finally wants
To meet us
Face-to-face
And eye-to-eye—
As if we could even lift
Our voice?
Do you really think
That He will say
That you now
Have a choice?

That He's glad
You had more money?
That you could afford
A bigger house?
That you could leave
Your spouse and children
And not feel like a louse?
That you could have
All the sex you wanted
With whomever you pleased?
And love was something
Never considered important
As long as your wants
Were always appeased?

Do you really think
He cares more about your happiness
Than He does one soul?
And don't you think that He believes
That conception makes
A soul completely whole?

In the End
What will really matter?
What you had
Or didn't have before;
Or what you'll
Have forever
And will forevermore?

Someone Better Never Came Along

When I was five
I told my parents I hated them—
That I wished they both were gone,
But they never left me—
Someone better never came along.

When I was ten
My best friend thought
I liked someone more—
That his days as my friend were gone,
But both he and I remained best friends—
Someone better never came along.

When I was eighteen
My first girlfriend found another...
She said that I could be better than I was,
But since that time I have found
Someone better never came along.

When I was twenty-nine I married;
For what I hoped to be all life-long;
And despite each doubt
It has come about...
Someone better never came along.

All through my life
I have believed in God—
He has led me down the right path, on-and-on;
And yet, with all the opposition to Him
Someone better never came along.

Someone better never came along;
It has happened my whole-life-long;
For when you have the best
You passed each test, when
Someone better never came along.

Something of Value

Something of value;
Something of worth;
From conception to death
I pray my life is, on Earth;

A life that was worth living;
That touched another's heart;
That caressed another's soul—
Each and every part;

A life not just something owned;
Nor merely possessed;
But shared with another,
So we both feel blessed.

Sometimes something isn't really valuable,
Until you give it away.

Standing at the Cross

standing at the cross...roads winding brought me there;
standing at the cross...seeing pain, I knew I could not bear;
standing at the cross...God, made man, crucified above;
standing at the cross...who knew there could be such Love!

Stars

When the stars have been counted
One by one;
But before you get to the last
You've forgot where you'd begun;
It's time to admit
It doesn't matter how many;
What really does matter
Is that there's plenty
To go around—
One for each you and me;
To light-up the night—
Where dark used to be;
To show there is hope
No matter how black
Our lives sometimes seem
And there's no turning back;
Just imagine...the light
We see shining tonight
Began on its journey
Long before things weren't right;
It's as if God knew
When we had nowhere
To turn
We could always look up
And see that God's candles burn
Long into the night
And each following day;
And so it has been
Forever, some say;
And so it shall be
Wherever we roam
To remind us all
That God's always home.

The Beauty of the Bible

Feast your eyes
Upon the beauty of the Bible—
An opus of history and hope...
Of mystery and understanding;
Of reasons, seasons, scope;
A candle in a dark world—
Though worthless, unless lit;
A comfort for the lost and lonely;
A reason not to quit;
A memorial to the ages—
Each one recorded so
We would not lose our way,
Neither night nor day
Because we would always know
A parcel has been delivered
In payment for each sin;
Yet, in order to save...
Pain, death, and a grave—
Details detailed within;
A way to savor the Savior;
He's the twinkle in your eye...
Some think it's love,
But it's the One above—
He made this earth
In less than seven days
On His first try.

The Color of a Soul

The color of a soul
Can make us One
When we finally see
It has none.

The Edge of Water

Water has an edge to it,
Which can cut
To a mountain's core;
Yet, when tears flow
They are so smooth
They soothe the soul—
Who could ask for more!

Water has an edge to it,
Which is seamless—
Or so it seems;
Yet, each drop sparkles so,
You can't help, but know
Each one is full of dreams;

Water has an edge to it,
Which can conform to everyone;
For by the water's edge
We live and die—
And live again—
When baptized
Water's job is done.

Water is even more important than you think.

The Reason For The Season

Yes, Christmas time is coming
As it does every year;
But, yet, it seems its meaning
Is not so crystal clear
As was in the beginning
So very long ago
When Christ was born a baby
More pure than Christmas snow.

Some think the Christmas season
Is just for girls and boys;
Or giving/getting presents
And Santa Claus with toys;
It seems some have forgotten
That Jesus is the One
That Christmas has been named for—
God's only, precious, Son.

The reason for the season
Is Jesus Christ our Lord;
Not Santa Claus or presents;
Or gifts we can't afford;
The reason for the season
Is Christ, the child born;
So long ago to save us—
Not toys on Christmas morn.

The reason for the season?
God cared enough to give
His Son for our salvation
That we might with Him live;
The reason for the season—
No matter where we roam—
God claims us all His children
And wants to bring us Home.

The season has a reason—
To thank God for His love;
To offer our repentance
And pray to God above
We not forget the reason
Christ came to earth for all—
To be our one Redeemer
And save us from our "Fall".

The Things That Rein Dear

'Twas the night before Christmas
When all through the land
Most people were working...
Wasn't it grand!
Yet, all the stockings were hung
From the mantel with greed
So we could get what we wanted—
Not what we need.

And I in Miami and "Mom" in St. Paul—
Our recent divorce having divided it all—
Had both settled down
For a good winter's sleep
But I ended up dreaming
Of promises I didn't keep;

So I got up, read the paper—
Did so till nearly morn—
And learned a baby's not human
Until it is born?

That pornography's great—
It's free speech, after all?
And we all must accept both—
It's the LAW, after all...?

Seems the kind of person you are
Doesn't matter you see
Because if I expected you to be good
You'd have the right to expect good from me.

But then out in the yard
I heard such a beef
I jumped up, got my gun
To scare off the thief;

I unbolted the door,
Turned off the alarm
And carefully snuck out
To avoid any harm.

The haze from pollution
Blocked most of the moon's light
But I soon had the subject dead in my sights;
But before I could fire
It occurred to me
The fellow in red was just making
A delivery;
It wasn't a truck of UPS
And though his coat was red
It wasn't a van, either,
Of Federal Express;

It was just a small home
Pulled by things that used to rein dear
That tugged at my memory and heart
As their names called-out I did hear:
"On Honor, on Peace, on Hope, Responsibility;
On Faith, Love, and Life; and onward Family."

As dreams before waking
Fade when we open our eyes
The fellow in red
Slowly dissolved from disguise;
As he removed his hood
His face, I finally did see
And instead of seeing him
I was seeing me...

Not the me I was now—
No, not tattered and worn—
But unspoiled, happy, secure...
Like the day I was born.

There was peace in my eyes
Shining like the Christmas star
And my Dad's medal of honor I held close—
He had died in our war;
There was hope for my future
As far as I could see
And I welcomed the challenge and rewards
Of responsibility;
My faith was in God
And not this world's lies;
And not just my life was special
But all's—
From their conception
'Til their demise;

And I loved my country—
We were all Americans, you see—
And not just a collection
Of every nationality;

And my family was with me;
Where else would they be?
For all things that rein dear
Are for them—
Don't you see...

I awoke with a start;
All figures had gone away;
But the gifts left for us
Still last till today;

I got back with my wife—
She had the same vision that night;
And our family's together—
Everything is all right...

I don't travel as much—
40 hour's enough;
I found that time is more special
Than any new stuff;

We go to church every Sunday;
When we're not there we still pray;
And we remember and honor the past—
It's still important today;

And each day we value
What makes Christmas so clear—
It's not Santa Claus—
It's the things that rein dear.

The Times I Don't Remember

The times I don't remember—
From birth till five years old—
I find myself reliving
As my children's lives unfold...

When I tuck you into bed at night
My mind goes back to the time
When I was in your place
But knew not words, nor rhyme;

The things I am doing now for you
My parents did for me
But it's only now I understand
It's only now I see;

From tucking you into bed at night
To helping you say your prayers
I picture myself in your place
With MY parents standing there...

And although I never thanked them
For all they did, when I was small,
I'll now try to thank them daily
By giving you my ALL.

There is No Flake Like a Snowflake

There is no flake
Like a snowflake—
This I cannot comprehend!
Not one snowflake is like another!
When will this madness end?
Or, is it the pure genius
Of a God, who knows that we,
Too, do not want to be like another;
So, special we will be...

And how is this pure genius?
Because each one of us is the same;
Yet, each one of us is different;
And if not,
We have only ourselves to blame...
For copying another—
A thing snowflakes cannot do—
So, why don't you
Keep being like a snowflake
And
Keep being only you.

To Be, Or Not to Be, a Man

Born
With great expectations
From those who mattered most—
Yes, of course, my parents,
But more so, Father, Son, and Holy Ghost;
And those who went before me
And made this nation great—
The Fathers of our country...
The Founders of these United States...

There was a time, when men were men
Who did what they were supposed to do—
To love and honor parents
And defend this nation, too;

Who married for a lifetime;
Who raised sons constantly
To be everything that they could;
To appreciate what it meant to be free—

Not free from obligation;
Not free from responsibility;
Not free from knowing right from wrong;
Not free from understanding decency...

But free to defend women;
Free to believe God loves big and small—
That free to pursue happiness,
Yet, have both life and liberty,
Applies to not just one, but all...

Men believed that sex and love
Went hand-in-hand—
That one should not happen without the other—
That children are the most important thing in life—
Right after their Mother;

That pornography may be free speech,
But not for real men;
Who know what you choose to see,
Becomes who you are;
And the words, which you read and hear, reappear
In actions you cannot defend;

From conception through eternity
A man will provide, and love, and care,
But a man is only seen as a man
When he is All Ways there.

To Get a Life

To get a life
You must give a life—
The catch is
It must be your own...
It matters not
If it is a life of devotion
Or
Merely prayers
When you are alone;

It may be a decision
To keep the baby—
No matter how
It might affect your life;
It may be the choice
To stay together
Despite troubles
With your husband
Or your wife;

To get a life
You must realize
The one you have
Is, for you, the best—
God gave you yours
As a gift...
All He asks is
You treat it like it's blessed.

In order to really get a life
You need to realize
The one you have
Is the one
Which should be
Worth the most to you.

We Lead Our Life as The Light

We lead our life
as the light, faded,
when we are timid
to the core;
When we are afraid
of the future
and can't take it anymore;

We lead our life
as the light, glowing,
when hope shines
in our eyes;
When we begin
to look forward
to the future
as the sun does
each sunrise;

We lead our life
as the light, shining—
there for all to see—
when we lead others
from their darkness—
sharing our faith
in God's eternity;

If not...
we lead our life
as the light...extinguished.

We often cannot see
because we do not realize
we have chosen
to close our eyes.

Whatever Happened

Whatever happened
To the belief we once had
That there was good
And there was bad?

Whatever happened
To plain, common sense?
It's no longer plain
And things rarely make sense.

When we sleep now at night
We're more awake than asleep;
We dream that we're working
Or trying to keep
Promises to our kids
That we'll play with them soon
But the bills have to be paid—
The home loan's a balloon.

When we look back
From the future
Will we like what we see?
Will our memories fade
Because we had no time free
For memory-making
And the times we recall
Are from TV and tapes
And not our lives at all?

Is freedom so wonderful
When anything goes?
Does it improve our lives
Or add to our woes?

Just ask parents
Whose children
Want all in their sight
And if they don't get it
They fuss and they fight
Till their parents give-in;
There's no time to relax;
So they give-in to their kids
To get them off of their backs.

But when we give-in to our kids
Or anyone, for that matter;
We're saying to them
That our words are just chatter;

Our values are shallow;
Our beliefs insecure;
And as for what
They'll be in the future
We're really not sure.

What was right is now wrong?
And what was wrong is now right?
When freedom is free
Is it worth it to fight
For what we believe?
Well, it's anyone's guess
But if you ask me
The answer is "Yes".

When I Was Young

When I was young
I didn't make the rules—
They were already there
To follow—
They weren't made by
fools;
They were made by my
parents
And their parents before;
They were passed-on to
me
To follow
And not ignore;

They set boundaries
And limits
Expectations
And Goals
Responsibilities
Virtues
Values
And Roles
That I should pursue—
Try my best
To follow—
Because
What they stood for
Was solid;

Not superficial
Or hollow;
But now
I am older
And all that
Has changed,
But not for me—
Life
Still is arranged;

There is Love
There is Marriage
There is Family
And more...

There is working
And money,
But it's not
What I live for—

There is God
There is Jesus—
To me
They are One—
They're Salvation,
Forgiveness—
A True
Father and Son.

When The Mourning Comes

When the mourning comes
preceded by
no advance notice...
no one called
to warn us
and no one even wrote us
to prepare us
for a future
without someone
who we thought
always would be there...
we might not even know them
yet, somehow, we both
share...
a life, a love, an interest...
a belief, a country, or a song...
one moment
all was right...
the next
nothing could be
more wrong...

When the mourning comes
it might sneak-up on us...
catch us unawares...
make us think
we are alone...
make us think
nobody cares...

Or
it might
just be there...
a wave of emotion
crashing against our soul—
one instant we are half—
we are no longer whole...

What we need
at such a time as this
is more than
just a ray of hope...
more than
just a memory—
a short-lived way to cope...
What we need is faith
that the one we lost
isn't gone—
that their soul is saved
and their life
will continue on...

When
we, too,
believe
that
Jesus is the One...
and will rise like the Son...
when the mourning comes.

Why is Life More Important When It's Gone?

A classmate of my daughter died...
Life for my daughter will never be the same...
She went to the funeral home—
The first one, where someone her age was laid-out...
That night she couldn't sleep
So she crawled into bed with her younger sister...
Something she had not done for a long time...
And sleep finally came
But the memories still linger
And she will never be the same...

They say
Teenagers think they will live forever
But forever seemed a lot further away
Than it does now...

I cannot imagine
Being in those parents' place...
But I know if you believe in God and Jesus
Somehow the pain and grief can be replaced
By hope and anticipation
By longing, with an end in sight—
The future now has a new meaning
Although the present is not as bright...

Why is life more precious
When it is taken away?
If this is true
Then why is it
Abortions still occur each day?
Is it the fact that we did not get to choose
Which makes it so upsetting?
That makes no sense at all...

It is the lives of others
Which make us happy...
It is the reason we live as we do...
I am special, it's true
But not more than you
Yet, we still act like
We don't have a clue.

Why Was My Life Taken?

Why was my life taken
Before I was ready?
Was it because I might not ever be?
Because my faith, now sure and steady
Wouldn't be there to lead and direct me?
The world would have ridiculed
And forsaken
My need for hope in a hopeless world?
Now, despite so many hearts now aching
I rest in a blanket of love, unfurled.

I wish I could comfort you
Like I am comforted;
Please know I remember only you.
You did your best...
Jesus did the rest;
Heaven, indeed, is true.

Wish No More

We have all been wished a Merry Christmas,
Happy Holidays, Season's Greetings;
And the warmth of the words
Touches our souls
At each and every meeting;
The friendships re-established
Make celebrations bright,
But Christmas has always meant
More to me than behaviors based
Upon just one day and night...

And so I wish for you to wish no more—
For each sin has been forgiven...
And more than merry should be felt...
For we've been given Heaven;
And friendships now can become happy celebrations
For an eternity
For on Christmas,
As each warmed soul knows,
Jesus came
To save both you and me.

Without God

Without God...
The words strike fear in me
More than anything
I can imagine...

Although
I don't even like
To think about it,
I can imagine
Coping with life
Without my wife—
My love, my life,
My everything—
Easier than I can
Without God...

Without God
Love
And life
Seem impossible...

Without God
I would not be here;
You would not be here;
Our children would not be
Here...
Everything...
Everything that makes life life
Exists because of God...

Supposedly intelligent people
Tell others
There is life
Without God...
What kind of life?
Life with no Faith...
No Forgiveness...
No Future...

How can someone even
Imagine
The Earth
Going out into space
And coming back
Along the same route
Each and every year
Without variations?

If
The same degree of perfection
Existed here on Earth
That existed
In the Earth's orbit
No one would ever
Miss a putt in golf;
No one would miss
A spare in bowling—
There would be
Only strikes...

This type of perfection
Would make life boring—
God's perfection
Makes life possible...

If man was in control
Of the Earth's orbit
We wouldn't last...
Have you ever flown
On an airplane?
Have you ever driven
On an expressway?
Have you ever been
Consistently
On time
Or
Where you wanted to be

When you wanted to be?
Have you ever felt safe?

So safe
That you
Didn't even have to
Think about it?

Think about it...
Safe like you feel
Each day
When the sun rises...

Safe like you feel
When the sun sets
And you know
It won't
Be the last time...

Safe like you feel
When you see
The seasons change...

When a spring rain falls...
When crops grow...
When leaves turn colors...
When snow falls...
When snow melts...
When a spring rain falls...

As safe as you felt
In your parent's arms
As a child...

It is nothing
Compared
To how safe you are
In Gods arms—

Arms which encircle
Earth's orbit
And keep it
Safely in place...

Arms which encircle
The earth
And keep it
Just the right distance
From the sun...

Arms which encircle
The earth
And keep water
From escaping,
Or even
Ever being consumed,
But rather,
Constantly recycled
With no loss at all...

God recycles perfectly—
Think about it...
Arms which
Embrace us
If we let Him
And
Even when we don't...

Life
Without God...
Is that what we want?
Is that all we can imagine?
Is that even possible?
I don't think so.

Worth Fighting For

There once was a time
When we had values
Worth fighting for—
For keeping
For right
For evermore...

Worth defending
From destruction
From losing
From wrong;
From weakness
From violence
From division
From strong
Opponents to freedom
That's never been free
'Til now
When I's more important
Than you, us, or we;

We used to have
Things in common;
We used to have beliefs
On which we'd agree;
We used to want the same things
And those things were not
The kind of things you can see...

Well, actually you could—
Those things were actions of love;
Of hopes for the future;
Reflections of God above;
Things we said to each other
And things we would never say;
Things we always strived for

And prayed for
And we lived life that way...
Sure, money was important,
But not important as life—
Be it a husband's, a child's,
An unborn's, a wife;

Once I would die for what I believed
And you would die
For what you believed, too;
You would die for me
And I would die for you;

But now, it is Now—
We don't believe the same
And dying's the last thing we'd do—
You see, life is a game
That we must win
At any cost
But in the end
If we win every Thing
Isn't Everything lost?

Our values?
Our morals?
Our very soul?
When all we are is Have
Can we ever be Whole?

Am I speaking of couples?
Of family?
Or our country?
It doesn't matter,
You see
For what goes for One
Goes for all Three.

You Touched My Heart When You Were Born

Sweet Sixteen...
At times the words don't even seem
To belong
In the same universe...
At other times
There could be
No better match;
Especially for a Father...
How the years have flown
And how you have grown;
What do I want you to know
Today and every day
For the rest of your life
Besides what I know—
Everything (just kidding).

I know you sometimes never listen,
But that you always hear;
That you say that you don't care,
But then you wipe away a tear;
That you do not want to be like us,
But you watch everything we do...
That you don't believe in what we say,
But you can see we believe in you.

You touched my heart when you were born;
That touch has not gone away;
Your fingers, toes, and pretty nose
Were in my life to stay;

You know I don't know all the answers,
But those I know are true...
Yes, there still is right and there is wrong;
And only One will do...

When it comes to love
I pray every day
You find love like I've known
That gives as much as it takes away;

I pray you someday love as completely
As your Mother loves us
And loves me;
I pray you have learned by watching
Both of us
What love is supposed to be...

And when I'm gone
I have a Friend
Who'll still watch over you...
He always has, He always will;
His love's even greater than
Mine for you...
Thank God... He's your Friend, too.

Pursuit of Happiness

Spring had arrived—just barely—as it often does here in Michigan. I was outside, in the backyard of my house, where I usually spend much of my time. Winter is usually much too long, and after being cooped-up indoors for four months, I need to get out as much as possible. Besides, there is always so much to do.

As I walked through the yard, in search of weeds, which needed pulling, and perennials which needed dividing, I glanced at the wren house I had built and put up two years prior. For the past two years I had had the pleasure of having a pair of wrens move in, set-up house, and raise a family. Wrens, for some reason, are one of my favorite birds. I am not sure if it is their diminutive stature, combined with their larger-than-life attitude; their constant fluttering about, looking for something to eat, or explore; or just their simple, yet cheerful, songs. Whatever the reason, I enjoyed them immensely, and the past two springs and summers were more enjoyable because of their presence.

This spring, however, they had not arrived yet, and I was worried, both for me and them. Me, because despite my love for solitude in my backyard, I still enjoyed the casual company they provided; and them, because after the past two years, I had become more attached to them, even though it was a one-sided relationship. Sure, I was their landlord, but were they even aware of that fact, and if so, did they care? I doubted it, but it did not matter.

As I continued to putter in the spring sunshine I noticed a small, brown, flying object land on one of the posts in my garden. It was indeed the long-anticipated arrival of the wrens, or should I say, wren, because there was only one. I looked and listened for the longest time, and the mate never showed up, despite the constant callings of the male wren (which I somehow knew it was), which were somehow different, more constant, and more urgent than I had heard in previous years. Nine notes...I made sure I counted them because it was an unusual song being sung this spring. Nine notes...over and over and over again, with only a brief pause for a breath, in-between each song...tweet, tweet, tweet, tweeeeet, tweet, tweet...tweet, tweet, tweet. Three quick, short tweets, a long tweet, two more quick tweets, a brief pause, and then three more concluding tweets. Then the same song repeated after only a second's rest. This, I quickly observed, went on non-stop, and continued all day, every day, and did so for the next two months.

The song began before sunrise and lasted until after sunset. Evidently the wren was calling for his mate, or any mate after awhile, because this song continued with the same intensity each day, as it had the first day. This search for a wife was so important that nothing else seemed to matter.

He did take time, however, to prepare the wren home for immediate occupancy, when his mate did arrive. He constantly collected small twigs and branches during his exploration of the yard; bringing them home and tucking them exactly where they belonged, in anticipation of her arrival. So much time eventually passed, however, that the twigs were sticking out the small entrance hole, and he had to remove some. There did, after-all, have to be room to raise a family.

After about a month, my love of wrens began to both decrease and increase. Decrease because my wife, Anita, and I usually slept with our windows open once the warm weather finally arrived in Michigan (about June), and the wren usually woke up and began his singing much sooner than we were willing, or able, to begin our day. And each day, until the first day of summer arrived, the sun came up a little earlier, resulting in even a longer day for the wren, and a shorter night's rest for us. We were eventually able to adjust, just like those people who live next to railroad tracks are able to filter out the noise of trains. By comparison, the song of a wren was not as loud, but it was more constant. His songs just became a part of our lives, as did the sunrise.

My love for wrens increased because of the same song and same behavior. How important this search for a wife was! Non-stop calling, non-stop preparations for making a home for a mate, whom he just seemed to know would be arriving, although, evidently, not soon. Keeping himself busy, and fed, and fit; Never feeling sorry for himself because of loneliness; Living life to the fullest, no matter what that might be that day, but obviously looking for more out of life than one little wren could provide for himself. We all need a goal in life—a reason for living. This little male wren had found one and was pursuing it to the fullest and to the best of his ability. It was the pursuit of happiness which was driving him. When he might find that happiness was uncertain. Whether he would ever find that happiness was unknown. Perhaps he would never be as happy as he hoped (assuming birds hope), but it did not matter, for he would make the best out that relationship as he could (who could doubt that) and that pursuit is what would make him, and most likely his mate, happy.

After more than a month of this constant singing had passed, I began to put words to the beat of the song...giving meaning to the call....putting myself into his place and imagining what I would be saying. Nine beats every 5 seconds. They sounded exactly the same, but were they? "I've built a home for you...where are you?" "This house was built for two—I need you." "I don't know what to do. Where are you?" "I need you to make my dreams come true."

Two months passed, since this singing, calling, yearning and hoping had begun, and still no response. No answer to his fervent song. This evening, as usual, I was out in the yard "working". I could take it no longer and I wondered how the little wren could go on, as well. He was the one doing all the work. I only had to watch and listen to him sing his little heart out. The only thing I knew to do was pray. God had said that he knows when a sparrow falls. The same must be true for wrens, too, but I did not want him to fall, nor fail, so I prayed a little prayer... "Please, God, could you please let this little wren find the mate he so desperately wants, needs, and deserves."

The very instant I finished my prayer the wren started singing much differently. His song was more excited and emotional, if there is such a thing in a bird's song. He flew quickly around the yard and then back to the little birdhouse he had furnished, continuing to sing loudly. A moment later, another wren arrived and landed next to him on top of the house. They sang back and forth for just a moment, and then she—it just had to be a she—entered through the hole in the front of the house and it just as quickly became a home. This moment definitely gave new meaning to the phrase, "He'll be singing a different tune." The female wren must have liked what she saw in the house, but more likely what she saw in this little male wren, for she decided to stay. They, too, raised a family, but they have never come back.

The memory of that spring and summer, as well as the 9-note melody, remain firmly attached in my memory, and I think about it, and them, every time I go in the backyard and see the little gray wren house still attached to the trunk of our tree.

To this day, I do not know whether it was my prayer for the bird, or the wren's prayer, which was answered. What I do believe is that it was the wren's dedication to life and determination to make the best of it, and never give-up, which both God and I responded to. The male wren's behavior let us both know that he would never give up...that he had both the faith and hope to continue, no matter what. It was just that both God and I seemed to make up our minds at the same time that something must be done, but only one of us was able to do something about it.

Royal

Royal wasn't a bad boy. He never got into any trouble that his parents couldn't get him out of. He had one problem, however, that bothered him sometimes, and he just did not know if he should do anything about it; he could not feel at all for other people. He didn't care what they thought about. He didn't care what they did. He didn't care if they were lonely, hungry or scared. Whatever other feelings other people might have, Royal just didn't give a darn. Being without feelings wasn't all that bad though. He never had to get involved to not feel guilty. He never lost a minutes' sleep thinking about someone else's emotional or physical problems. It didn't even bother him when he saw pictures of hurt or starving people on the TV. Ah, yes, TV. What a marvelous invention! Royal's parents had years before discovered the mesmerizing qualities that it had on little Royal. He ate his breakfast, lunch, dinner and countless snacks in front of all the numerous and varied characters on TV. When he took naps, he could only fall asleep if the sound from the television was in the background, and would wake-up screaming if anyone dared to come in and turn it off.

At first, Royal's parents took the time to monitor what shows he would watch. They explained to him that the people on the screen were just actors and if it looked like they got hurt or killed, they were just pretending and would show-up in a day or two on another station. Time for Royal started getting scarce for his parents, however, after they moved into a bigger house that they really couldn't afford without both of them working full-time. Thank God for TV! Royal didn't miss his parents a bit, as long as there was something good on TV, and now that they had cable, Royal was as happy as he thought he would ever be. So were his parents. Royal's parents never did get around to explaining the difference between fictional shows and the news that occasionally came-on, while switching channels. Royal figured those people were actors, too, and that whatever was shown or talked about would have a happy ending. If someone was hurt or killed they would appear on another station, as good as new, for as long as the people who wrote the stories wanted it to be that way. Just how or when Royal stopped caring, it is hard to say. After seeing so much death, destruction, violence and stupidity on TV for all his formative years and without the guiding- hand or mind of his parents to distinguish exaggeration from reality, Royal just sort of gave-up caring. It never really ever made a difference how he felt about what he saw or heard on TV. The outcome was already determined. When reruns appeared he realized it even more... the ending was always going to be the same.

The first day of kindergarten the first words out of Royal's mouth were "Where's the TV?" Upon being informed by his teacher that television sets were not allowed in the classroom, Royal promptly walked out and had to be forcibly returned by his parents. That first day of school was the longest day of young Royal's life. It was longer than "Gone With the Wind" and "Alice in Wonderland" combined. Or so it seemed. Royal spent all that first day watching the other children and teacher. He pretended they were characters in an episode of "Mr. Cooper". He couldn't change the channel, but at least there were no commercials. When Royal got home that afternoon, the first thing he did was turn on the television set and turn up the volume all the way so he couldn't hear his mother ask him how his day was. He didn't eat his dinner and went to bed early, without even looking at the local listings. His parents knew something was wrong, but they were not sure what, or even how to find out, since Royal never had time to talk because he was always too busy watching something.

His parents went into the den and turned on their TV set hoping Doctors Ruth, or Brothers or "Laura" had something relevant to say. It was rough being a parent. Never knowing what to do and never knowing for sure, which channel to watch to find out.

That evening Royal was awakened from his sleep by what he thought was the growling of his stomach. He had never gone to bed hungry before and his tummy was telling him to do something about it...or so he thought. After rubbing his eyes, he looked around his room and discovered that his door had disappeared; and the window too. There was no light on in the room, but there was an eerie glow similar to that coming from his parents room late at night, after they had fallen asleep and forgotten to turn-off their TV. Royal knew he should be scared, but somehow he felt very comfortable there; especially with the soothing humming sound coming from his aquarium pump. It sounded just like a television set that was between stations. He closed his eyes and tried to go back to sleep, but his imagination took over and he thought to himself, "I'm going to pretend that I'm inside a TV." And so he did, but he didn't have to pretend hard at all because he was inside a television set; he just didn't know it, yet. He soon figured it out, however, when he heard his parents getting up and walking towards his room. He heard them say that they wanted to see some news show on Channel 3. Then he heard a loud click and one of his walls suddenly became a giant window and he could see his parents in their pajamas looking at him. But, they couldn't see him. It was like they were looking right at him, but seeing someone or something else. They never even heard him, when he yelled and screamed for them to come into his room and get him. This was getting serious. It was almost time for "Jerry Springer". But then he thought, "This is kind of neat. I'm on the inside looking out for a change and my parents don't even know I'm here."

He decided to take full-advantage of this unique opportunity. He thought, "Instead of watching television today, I'm going to watch my parents, without them even knowing it. This is going to be great!"

And so it was for a time... Royal never had gotten a chance to observe his parents that closely before. The only time he could remember was after he was just born and his parents were trying to establish "bonding", whatever that was. At least that's what his parents told him they were doing in the picture he saw of him looking into his parent's eyes. They had heard about it on "The Family Channel". Anyway, there was Royal looking deep into his parents' eyes for the second time in his life and they didn't even see him. Somehow that disturbed him momentarily, but he shrugged it off and got on with his newest TV in reverse show that he decided to give the name of "TV in Reverse". "Another World" was already taken. Royal could tell his parents weren't really involved in the show they were watching because they started talking to each other. He decided to listen to them talk. That was something he rarely had time to do. What with his sleeping, eating and television watching, there just was not enough time left. Well, maybe just enough to go to the bathroom occasionally and other necessities.

His parents were quite interesting, he found out that morning. His father talked about his job, and Royal finally found out what his dad did when he left the house every day. He was an engineer at Ford. Royal never even knew that Ford made trains. It must be a secret project or something because he thought he had seen all their commercials and he had never seen one about a train. Maybe Royal could get a ride some day. His mother, Royal discovered, was a manager at a temporary-help agency. Royal knew the only kind of help anyone ever got around home was temporary, so why should it be different anywhere else. After awhile the subject-matter started to

get serious. They were actually talking about removing all the television sets in the house and replacing them with, of all things, books. How could they even think about taking such a drastic measure? Why? For what purpose? What could it possibly accomplish? And most importantly of all, what was Royal supposed to do instead of watching TV. What else in the whole, wide world could be so important? As Royal listened, he began to find out the reasons for his parents' feelings. "I'm worried about Royal", his mother said anxiously. "Why? What seems to be wrong with him? He's all boy isn't he?" his father replied proudly. Royal smiled from ear to ear when he heard his father call him, "All boy".

That's all he ever wanted to be in life—someone his father would be proud of. He had heard stories about how wild and reckless his dad was when he was small. It always sounded like it was something his dad was proud of, so it must be a worthwhile goal in life to be that way. He figured that was why his parents never disciplined him, when he was bad; and why he always seemed to get his way as long as he protested loud enough and hard enough. As a last resort, he found crying usually got him what he thought he wanted, when all else failed.

"I'm just not sure if we are raising Royal to be a good person," His mother continued. "He just seems to be totally obsessed by the television set lately and I'm not so sure that the shows he watches are having a positive effect on his personal and emotional development." "Huh?" his father muttered. "I'm sorry. I was listening to what Jenny was saying about how to have safe sex, without your parents finding out because they might ground-you and not let you ride your bike for a week." "That's what I'm talking about," his mother sputtered. "Huh," his dad replied. The conversation went back and forth all morning, with Royal listening intently to every word. He found out many things he never knew about before. Like that his mother was pregnant and was worried about having to stop working and not being able to afford to keep the new house. Royal thought, "Why doesn't she just get an abortion?" Royal wasn't sure what a 'bortion was, but he knew having one solved people's money problems on TV shows. And after his mom's money problems were over, she could have the baby and stay home with the new baby and Royal. That would be nice.

His dad, Royal realized, was not very happy with his job at Ford. "Who wouldn't be happy driving a train?", Royal wondered. His dad was even thinking about quitting. "Hey Dad!" Royal yelled. "Dads never quit on TV." But his dad didn't hear him. Both of Royal's parents started looking very sad and Royal felt very uncomfortable watching them get upset. It was not at all like how he felt about the actors on television when they were crying or hurt. I mean, they were just pretending on all those soaps and news shows, weren't they? "Hey, wait a minute!" Royal yelled to himself. "Maybe it is true that television is made-up of all kinds of people pretending to be in all kinds of situations. And maybe they are trying to make us believe they are experiencing all the different feelings they act-out; but maybe someone, somewhere actually does feel or act that way. Maybe some people actually do get hurt or killed. Maybe others are really starving to death somewhere in the world. And what if that little boy's parents on the news show last night were really killed by that truck..."

Royal started to cry; for real this time. And he was scared and lonely; and for the first time in his life the humming of the TV did not comfort him. All he wanted was to be held and hugged by his parents and to hug them back and never let go. As he was rubbing the tears from his eyes, he heard a loud click and when he looked up, his doorway had reappeared and both of his parents were coming in through it. Royal jumped up to meet them and they hugged each other for a long, long time. None of the TV sets came on for the next month. Instead, Royal's parents read him books and they talked about all the things Royal had ever seen on television shows, and was unsure about. Maybe it was two months that the TVs were off.

Royal's mother had a little baby girl and his father took a cut in pay, so he could spend more time with his family. They sold their big house and moved into a small home; and now they only watch television, when they can all watch it together.

Stone

Whenever time passes
As always it does
We seem to ignore it
Or at least that's how it was
Until that morning of mornings
When so very nearby
I heard a small scream
Or was it a cry?

Upon closer inspection
I found a small stone
So very afraid
So very alone;
Yes, times had been hard
As I'm sure you might guess
For if you were a stone
Could you expect less?

The stone blabbered and muttered
It sobbed and it grieved
But it finally did stop
Boy, was I relieved!
The stone said he'd fallen
From a mountain nearby
And I just had to help him
Return close to the sky...

Where the friends he grew-up with—
The birds and the bees
The grass and the flowers
The clouds and the trees
Called for his return
But what could he do?
He didn't have legs
Like me, or like you;

He couldn't walk, run, or jog
Or stand alone;
He only could roll;
Remember, he was a stone.

Somehow I felt sorry—
Now don't ask me why;
I even thought I might help him
Return toward the sky;
But a stone had never helped me;
Except to let me throw
One at a can
And once I dropped one on my toe;
Still I couldn't imagine
What was in it for me?
Sure favors are cheap
But should they be free?

So I asked him politely
If I helped him return
What would I get?
What would I earn?

The stone seemed to quiver
As it thought of a prize
Worthy of someone
Like me, who was wise
Enough to return him
To the home he once knew
On top of that mountain
Near the sky, oh, so blue.

After a moment
The stone spoke again
For he'd thought of a gift
To give me right then;

Did I know where stones came from?
And I had to admit
That I really had never
Thought about it;

So a deal was made
For though I'd not thought of it before
It now bugged me no end
And I had to know more;

I put the stone in my pocket
He said his name was "Hard".
I asked, "To pronounce?"
He said, "No! "H", then "ard". . . .
On the journey upward
He talked about how
Stones do not come from nowhere
But I had to vow
To promise to always
Repeat what I'd hear
About where stones come from—
How they appear;

He said stones, unlike people,
Are old when they're smaller;
That when he was younger
He had been taller
Than the mountain we climbed...
I asked, "How can that be?"
He said, "Be quiet and listen
And then you shall see
That stones, although small,
Have seen much — this is why—
They may not get around much
But life passes them by. . . ."

He recalled his beginning . . .
He simply was there
And it really was dark
So he didn't know where;

Then a voice he heard
It said, "Let there be light."
And he finally could see;
Boy, was it a sight!
Then the voice spoke again
For the water to split;
Half went to the sky
But the rest? He stayed under it.

Till the voice came again
Said, "Let dry ground appear."
And he rose to the sky;
Well, at least very near;
The voice told things to grow
Each and every place;
He found he had bushes and trees
All over his face.

Then the voice made the sun
The same one seen today
To make the light
To make the day.

Then the voice made the moon
To help light the night;
It looked as big as the sun
But it wasn't as bright.

The voice echoed again
Made all creatures alive;
Fish, mammals, and birds—
They all did arrive;

Hard said,
"They made homes in my bushes
Ate fruit from my trees;
Oh, yeah, that reminds me
There were insects and bees;
And snakes, frogs, and toads
And before I forget;
There were dinosaurs, too;
Some dry and some wet."

"Then the last thing the voice did
Was make a woman and man
Although not in that order
But both then began
To live in a garden

The voice had made
Till they did something wrong
And became afraid."

What happened then
Hard couldn't say
For when the voice got loud
He got blown away;
Into pieces of mountain—
Yes, as he had become older
He found that he, too
Had become a little boulder.

He saw many moons
And many a sun
With a collection of friends
Who weighed many a ton;
Then it started to rain
So long, he got downhearted
For before it had stopped
He was back where he'd started...
Under the water

As dead things floated by
Making him sad
Making him cry.

Hard said,
"I was all alone
And wished I could float
When overhead
I saw a large boat;
It came closer and closer
When finally
I rose out of the water
And the boat settled on me."

"Then a miracle happened
At least that's how it seemed
For all I'd seen drowned, now lived...
All I'd hoped for and dreamed

Had somehow come true...
I was no longer alone
Pairs of all things that lived—
Two of everything known
Got off of that boat
Passed before me to see
It was like a parade
Given only for me."

"Then the sky filled with colors
I'd not seen there before
They curved all together
And it's never rained like before
But each time I see them
Even up to today
I'm reminded how special
Are all the things that came my way. . ."

"That was far from this place
And I'm sure that you must
Wonder how I got here
So I hope that you trust
My *rockcollections*—
Scratched in my surface alone;
Yes, it is true—
They are etched in stone."

"As you may remember
I once was a boulder
But I became smaller
As I became older."

"The wind and the rain
The cold and the sun
Molded my characteristics—
Each and every one;
Small droplets of water
Sometimes soaked into me
And then, when they froze
I became all
I was cracked-up to be."

"I've been ballast in boats
Catapulted in wars
Made into stone soup
And held open doors;
I've been picked up and carried
And then tossed aside
When a stone brighter than me
Got picked-up and tried."

"Two stones are too heavy
To tote very far
So one often is left
Under the star
That makes the day
That the voice made;
I've only heard it once since
But I'm sure that it's stayed
Close to this world
That I've been around
For wherever I look
I always have found
The things it first made
And that includes me
And nothing has changed
Too drastically . . ."

"Except that first man and woman's
Heirs seem to have forgotten
They are here to control
Not to make rotten
The things the voice made—
Things like you and like me—
From the air in the sky
To the depths of the sea."

"Remember," Hard said,
"I heard that voice just once more?
It was long ago
But the words still me implore. . ."

"I was on the side of a road
When a man took hold of me
And held me up high
For others to see;
Then the same voice I'd heard
On the day I was made
Echoed from the man
But I was not afraid."

"It said if others were silent
And held their voice
The stones would cry-out—
I did not have a choice;
From that instant on
I knew I could talk
But like the voice said,
Only if others balk."

"Well, that day must have come
For you heard me today
I'm sorry I scared you
But there was no other way
To get your attention;
I have to start now
Spreading the Story
But I don't quite know how."
"So if you help me travel
From here back to where
I came from at first
I know that we'll share
The greatest adventure
Either of us has known
And we'll have each other
So we won't be alone."

So what could I do?
What could I say?
Except to agree—
Stones don't talk every day.

The Womb With a View

Why Mary's skin had no pigment in it, was never known, but it offered to the medical professional the chance to observe first-hand the miraculous workings of the human body; things that could only be figured-out through autopsies and the examination of dead bodies. Some biological activities can be discovered during operations, but only for limited time-periods, and never for a long enough time to suit those interested in truly understanding how a human body works.

Mary's skin was as clear as glass; just like those of glass fish you see occasionally in aquariums. Fortunately, for Mary, only parts of her body were that way; parts that she could cover conveniently with clothing. Her face, arms, hands, legs, and feet were of normal coloring. It was primarily her torso that was clear enough to reveal all that went-on inside.

Despite her obvious peculiarity, she had been able to lead a somewhat normal life, due mainly to her parents most conscientiously guarding her privacy, all her life. Other than her parents, only her family physician had the chance to see Mary in person and up close. Over the years he had been allowed to take pictures, and even videos, of Mary's insides, but he always managed to conceal both his and Mary's true identity, whenever he made his findings public.

Mary's social life was quite limited by her condition. All through high school she had to be excused from any physical education classes because she was not allowed to use a public shower, where others might see, but not understand, her body. And when summer came she had to be especially careful that the sun did not penetrate into her body through her clear skin. Internal organs were not made to withstand the heat, or the solar radiation. Without the protection of normal layers of skin, Mary would die due to overheating, or damage from the sun.

One summer though, Mary did meet someone; someone who understood her problem and who would not reveal it to anyone else. His name was Joe, Mary's doctor's son. He had been going away to school for the last seven years and had occasionally come in contact with Mary at his father's office. They never really had the time to get to know each other very well, due to Joe's schooling and Mary's desire for privacy, but every time their eyes met they never immediately looked away.

This summer Joe was going to be an intern with his father. Joe had, through the years, picked up a lot of his father's beliefs about the practice of medicine; That everyone, regardless of their age, race, or income level, had the right to be treated with respect and dignity, when it came to their medical problems. Insurance, or lack of it, had no bearing on how well someone was treated. If enough money came in each month, so that the bills could be paid on time, and there was enough money left over to live on, then that was all that was important. As long as the office could remain open to serve the needs of the community, then Joe's father felt he was a success.

Joe never assumed for an instant, any time in his young life, that his dad was anything, but a success. A lot of Joe's friends in medical school felt differently about that though, and whenever Joe happened to mention his dad and his practice to them, they were sure to let him know.

After awhile Joe realized that they weren't really his friends, after all; and they stopped associating with him after too many differences of opinion about why they were going to become doctors. Joe wanted to help people, while they wanted to make a lot of money and become rich and famous, or at least rich.

Joe really needed a friend the summer he was to help his dad. He needed someone besides his dad to talk to about his feelings because most of his feelings revolved around his dad. Joe thought he had his priorities straight, but he just needed someone to listen to him think out loud.

The first day of work, Joe met Mary again. And again, when their eyes met, they remained fixed on each other for the longest time.

"Joe! Joe! Wake up!" his dad said.

"What?" Joe replied.

"Joe, I want to introduce you to my favorite patient, Mary Singleton," Joe's dad replied.

"Glad to meet you Mary," Joe responded.

"Nice to meet you, too," Mary meekly answered. And with that simple exchange began the start of the most meaningful relationship either Joe or Mary had ever known.

Mary and Joe spent every free moment together. There weren't many of them, but what time they had together was the best either of them ever had with anyone.

For her whole life, Mary never once was able to feel totally normal. Every night before bed, when she looked into her full-length mirror, she was both disgusted and amazed with her body. No one else had one like it—it was certain, but Mary never could understand why God would do something like this to someone like her.

Mary had many sleepless nights suffering from indigestion, due to her feelings, but she always tried to make the best of every situation—even the uncomfortable ones. There aren't, after all, too many people who can see their stomach growl.

If Mary couldn't thank God for her body, she most surely could thank Him for Joe. Joe made her feel normal, and in doing so, he accomplished more than Mary ever thought possible. Joe knew all about her body. He understood her need for privacy. And most of all, he cared a lot about her and that caring slowly, but surely, turned to love; and that is where this story really begins...

Mary and Joe dated every chance they got. Being an intern, however, did not allow Joe many free moments, but those he did have, were spent with Mary.

One of those moments, however, changed her life, and Joe's life, forever, but fortunately she recorded many of the personal details in her personal diary, and now, I have her permission to share those memories with you...

Day 28 (After conception—We only did it once!):
I should have seen it coming. Somehow, that line sounds funny, but it really isn't. I'm afraid I am pregnant. I know my body all-too-well to not know when something is wrong, and something is definitely wrong now. No period for two months and I feel better than I ever have before. I know I should go to see Dr. Fine, but I really want to wait and see, and when I say see, I really do mean see.

Day 29:
I must have stood in front of my mirror today for more than an hour. My Mom knocked on the door and about scared me to death. I haven't told her or my dad, yet, but I really want to tell Joe first—even before Dr. Fine. So much to think about and so much to do, but I have to start somewhere, and Joe is the best place I know.

Day 30:
I saw Joe last night, and when I told him I thought I was pregnant, he slowly smiled the biggest smile I have ever seen him smile; he then laughed and grabbed me with both arms firmly around my waist, swung me around once, quickly; but then slowed down, until it felt like we were dancing. Tears filled my eyes, and his, too, and I just knew everything was going to be all right; even before he said those very words. Joe said I should go see his dad, just to be sure; and then said that he would go with me to tell my parents. My parents loved Joe, but this was before this had happened, and I really did not know what they would say or do, but I knew I did not want to do it alone.

Day 31:
I saw Dr. Fine today, and, yes, he did say everything was fine, and would be fine...and, oh, yes, that I was indeed about one month pregnant. It was a little embarrassing when he asked when I thought I might have become pregnant, and my mind wandered immediately back to the night at his apartment, with Joe nearly falling asleep after working 14 hours, but still cuddling me so close, until we were beyond close, and we just stayed that way until both Joe and morning came. Dr. Fine noticed the far-a-way look in my eyes, and knew the pregnancy was the result of love,

and, yes, he knew, without me telling him, that his son, Joe, was the father, and that, yes, everything would be fine.

Day 32:
I love my parents! I told them last night about me being pregnant and they really weren't that surprised, nor shocked. Even though they do not believe in sex before marriage, they do know how difficult it is to disassociate sex from love, and they feel, as I do, that all life is precious, and that definitely includes my baby's life. Baby...first time I have used that word. It sounds so right. Embryo and fetus just do not do life justice these days. And now that I think about it, justice does not do babies justice either. I could never abort this baby, and my parents never even thought about asking if I was going to keep it. It...so impersonal, and so inappropriate. Baby...my baby's temporary name will be Baby. I just looked down and introduced myself to Baby. She/he cannot hear me yet, but I know that Baby feels safe and warm, and I will have it no other way...not today, and not ever.

Joe was there, and he did look very uncomfortable, but my parents told both of us that everything in life happens for a reason, and if we believe in God, as we all do, then things work-out. My parents did not ask if we were going to get married, and they did not ask if we planned to put Baby up for adoption. I do think that they knew, as Joe and I did, as we looked into each other's eyes, that yes, we would eventually get married; and yes, we would keep Baby; and yes, everything would be fine.

Day 33:
Not sleeping much lately; So many things to think about. For one, Dr. Fine wants to continue to videotape my insides, but this time he wants to concentrate on my Baby. I want him to do this, too. Actually, before I went in to see him this morning, I knew that this is what I wanted. I must have been born the way I was for a reason more important than that of being just a window into a person's insides. I want the world to see that an embryo is a baby; a fetus is a baby; a baby is a precious life; and that all life is precious in not only God's eyes, but mine, too; and hopefully... eventually, everyone's eyes.

Another thing occupying my thoughts is Joe. He feels guilty about what has happened. I know he is happy, but I also know he knows I had other plans for my life besides being pregnant and taking care of a baby. Two years of community college were just to be the start of going to a 4-year college, and getting a degree in nursing, with the goal of being in charge of a maternity ward, of all things. Joe is 25 and I am 20, and the birth of our baby is only 8 months away. At least he is done with his education. Mine is only just beginning.

Day 34:
Before going to the Dr. Fine's office today, for my first official videotaping of my Baby, I remembered I had once written a poem about this very subject. It was so long ago that I had forgotten about it, until this morning.

About three years ago I had written a pro-life poem and posted it on the Internet. I have always been pro-life, and it just got to me that no one was really seeing things from a baby's point-of-view. I mean, everyone here on earth was given the opportunity to live, and yet they feel it is okay to deny that right to others; even their own baby.

I have always been shy and turned-off by all of the politics surrounding the issue, so I never really got involved in the whole pro-choice/pro-life debate, until I saw pictures of aborted babies on display at my college. God, how could someone/anyone do this to another human being! Not knowing what else to do to try and make my feelings known, and to, hopefully, make a difference in at least one person's life, I sat down and wrote this poem, not knowing at the time that I was writing about something that would eventually come true:

If You Could Just See Me

If you could just see me
Forming inside;
You'd witness a miracle
That some try to hide;
You'd see for yourself
That I'm made just like you;
God's method is tried;
God's method is true.

From conception,
Who I will become has been set;
There's naught you can do
To change who you will get;
Unless, you of course,
Decide to stop my growth;
But only Mom can decide, not Dad—
It doesn't take both.

I have just one chance to live—
I won't come again;
Till maybe in heaven we meet—
Only God can say when;
So please let me be born—
There is so much to do;
God creates life for All—
Not just me and you.

Life is a miracle.

Day 35:
Dr. Fine is going to post the videos he is making of my Baby and my pregnancy, on the Internet. He somehow is going to keep the source of the videos, and both his and my names a secret. I really hope so. I cannot imagine the unwanted publicity and attention my family, Joe, Baby, and I would receive if our identities became known. I am sure there will be some who will think this whole thing is a hoax, and just some special-effects movie, but that is out of my hands, and I am leaving it in God's hands from now on. I did, however, give Dr. Fine a name for the website: THEWOMBWITHAVIEW. He liked it.

Days 36-56:
I have written something for each day in my diary, but Baby is so small, you can hardly see him/her, yet. The website is up and running, and it has had thousands of hits a day. Most seem to just go to it out of curiosity, but some have left messages for us and others to see. Sure are some weird, hateful people in the world. I have stopped reading them. Most of the hurtful ones say this site is fake, or that I am committing a sin by doing it, or that I should be in a freak show at the circus. The positive ones said that it was about time someone actually saw what was involved in the creation of life, and that it was great that everyone finally could see what we each put our mothers through.

I have mainly just been recording my own physical and emotional feelings. I have, up to this time, been able to keep my pregnancy secret from everyone in the community; even my closest friends, but today someone finally guessed I was pregnant. Becky, a friend I have had since pre-school, came over to my house today and noticed I was getting a little chubby. I knew she could keep a secret (she never did tell anyone about the time I peed my pants at school in 2nd grade. She just splashed water on me at the drinking fountain, so that everyone would think that was why my pants were wet.), so I told her I was pregnant, and that Joe was the father. She wasn't that surprised, either. She said she thought something was up, since she saw me coming out of Dr. Fine's office quite a few times in the past month, and I did not work there, and I did not look sick. She did say she thought I might be visiting Joe, but sometimes his car was not in the parking lot, so she knew that could not be the reason I was there. Some detective that Becky is!

Day 57:
Baby is about an inch long now and his/her heart is beating so fast. By holding another mirror up to my full-length mirror I can see Baby quite well. Toes, fingers, arms, and legs are all forming. Who in their right mind would want to abort someone like this! I guess it really is true that there really is none so blind as those who will not see. People who choose not to see the truth, seem to make up their own "truths" to accommodate their special wants and desires. I really pray that all I am putting Baby and myself through is worth the effort.

Dr. Fine has been great and has told me I can quit this project whenever I want. I do sometimes wish I were normal, but in reality, I am. The only way I am different is that I can see what other people couldn't up till now. I just feel I was born for this reason; for this purpose; for this task. I told him I would let him know, but I also told him not to expect I would, and therefore, to stock-up on all the necessary digital equipment, including batteries. I would hate him, and others, to miss anything of importance, although every second somehow feels to be important to me.

Days 58-89:
Baby's growing and so am I. I am happy, but I cry a lot. Thank God for Guernsey's ice cream.

Day 90:
The website hits are up to 10,000 a day! I have seen articles in the news and tabloid headlines offering rewards for the identity of the womb-owner. It makes me nervous, but I trust everyone who knows.

Baby is about 3 inches long now, but I still can't tell if Baby is a boy or girl. Joe wants a healthy baby, and I want one, too. That is all that matters to us, and that is all that should matter to anyone.

The whole town now knows about my pregnancy. Not much I can do to hide that fact. For the sake of secrecy, I have lied about how far along I am, just to make it harder to have someone tie my pregnancy and that of the one on my website, together. Once I find out the gender of Baby, I will probably lie about it, or maybe just say I did not want Dr. Fine to tell me. Living in a small town has its advantages, but then again, everyone knows everything as soon as everyone else does. I do get the occasional stares, but more often than not I get words of encouragement, and questions about when the wedding will be. The wedding...Joe hasn't asked me to marry him yet. I know he has been busy at the clinic, and that this whole website thing is sort of freaking him out, despite the fact that he is a doctor, but I am at the point where I, too, am freaking out, and it is not so much about the pregnancy, as it is about Joe's silence.

Days 91-100:
Well, I know the sex of Baby, but like I said, I am not telling—even my diary. Dr. Fine has promised not to tell either, but otherwise, the whole world knows, or at least they can if they visit the website. Joe has been present for many of the video tapings of Baby and his/her development (thought I would give it away, huh.), so he, too, knows the sex of Baby. My mom and dad do not know. They want to be surprised.

The hits on the website are up to 50,000 a day! Other websites have arisen to take advantage of Baby's popularity. Some are taking bets about the birth date, while others are trying to track down the source of the videos. Some pro-choice sites have popped-up saying it is still not too late to have an abortion, and that this one pregnancy should in no way undo all the good that has been done for women since the Roe vs. Wade decision. Seems like no one ever mentions that probably one-half of the aborted babies were females. And what is wrong with males, anyway, that they, too, deserve to be aborted. Hormones definitely acting up again.

That placenta if definitely something I have not seen up close before. What a neat thing! Baby is about 5 inches long and is sucking and swallowing. What a cutie!

Day 101:
Joe just called from work and wants to meet me here, at my house, but he wants my parents to both be here, too. I wonder if

this is THE DAY he asks me to marry him? I will get back to you once I know...

Well, I am engaged. Joe was great. He apologized for waiting so long, but he said he just wanted to make sure I was sure about what I was doing with the whole Internet thing, and that he had wanted to marry me ever since the day he first saw me. That must have been when I was about 1year old, and I was in his father's office. I know I do not remember, but he said he does. We have decided to not get married until after the birth of Baby because we have not had sex since that one time, and being married would make it too hard (at least for him) to not want to have sex with me, and perhaps change the whole pregnancy experience. No real source for advice in this situation, but then again, first time for everything, but that second time is definitely something I am looking forward to.

Days 102-140:
I have gained so much weight it is ridiculous. Baby must be very happy in his/her wet, warm home. The website is among the most popular on the whole Internet, and the pressure to keep it a secret is enormous. Like being pregnant for the first time is not pressure enough. I have just now started to think about giving birth to Baby. Think I'll go throw up. Yep, I did. At least I lost some of that weight, but it will be back in a minute. Baby is about 10 inches long now! He/she also is starting to look like Joe. Be too bad if Baby was a girl. Kidding. I really do have a sense of humor about this whole thing. Without it I would crack up. As it is, I am laughing most of the time, except when I am crying or eating.

Day 141:
I felt Baby kick today. Must want out, but I am not going to let him/her. Being only one pound is no way to start life outside of the womb! I went to see Joe immediately, and he felt it, too. Somehow, seeing Baby, and having him/her touch you are two different things, but both are so neat, we just cannot control our feelings, and both of us cry and laugh a lot. We really have to watch what we say. It is almost impossible now to contain our joy and feelings about see our Baby grow. We want to tell the world, and not just show the world, what a baby means to parents who want a baby, and what it should mean to everyone.

Days 142-168:
We could make a ton of money off of this whole experience, but no one will ever know the identity of anyone involved, if I can help it. God must be watching over all of us, and He does know how much we can handle. Same old crazy comments, message boards and websites showing up. I don't read, or go to any of them because I am stressed enough, and I still need to plan our wedding. I am sure my Mom will be glad to help. She has been very supportive of me during this whole time, and neither she, nor my Dad has Internet access, anyway, so it is easy for them to keep away from all the potential distractions. They know I am doing what I feel I was born, and meant to do, and they are there for me.

I am gaining so much weight! It's amazing Dr. Fine can still see through me well enough to get clear pictures. He is amazing, too. Good thing, he, too, is a Christian, and a moral, honest person. Joe takes after him, in more ways than one. Joe's mom is not that aware of everything that is going on. It is not that she cannot be trusted, as much as it is that she does not want to know for fear of telling someone by accident.

Day 169:
Baby opened his/her eyes today and looked right at me. I swear he/she winked at me. I am sure it was water in his/her eyes. The first time in history that an unborn baby has seen his Mother! I am sure the reactions to this event on the Internet will be both wondrous, and disturbing, depending on if any of the viewers had ever had an abortion. I feel so sorry for them, but what could I do, besides hide the truth, which is something I just cannot do. At least with ultrasounds, the parents know the baby cannot see them, and that, I am sure, is somewhat comforting.

Life for me, and anyone else who will be watching on the Internet, will never be the same, and you do not know how happy that makes me feel, but I am sure it will take quite awhile for all of this to sink in, especially for those whose minds and hearts have been hardened by all of the untruths, misrepresentations, and filtered/censored facts through the past three decades. I am getting a headache. I want this to be over.

Day 170:
I did pull the plug—on the website. I just could not take it anymore, and ever since I saw Baby look at me, I just needed the bond that was being formed to be between Baby and me, and Baby and Joe, and no one else, I figured that everyone else would understand, and that they had seen enough to determine that an embryo, a fetus, an unborn baby, is a baby—a human being just like them; created just like them; with rights to Life, Liberty, and their own Pursuit of Happiness. Time will tell, but I just want to get on with a normal life, with Joe, and with my soon-to-be- born little Baby.

Days 171-266:
Well, I kept getting bigger and bigger, and so did Baby. The Internet kept running re-runs of the whole first 170 days on numerous websites, with our permission. Joe and I made plans for marriage the week after Baby was born. Everyone settled into a comfortable, private, life, and just let the pregnancy run its course.

Day 267:
Baby was born today at 3:17 A.M. (I wasn't sleeping, anyway). We gave Baby a new name. It was Iris. I know that probably sounds like the most unusual name in the world, but after looking her in the eyes for nearly the past 100 days, there was no other name that felt right.

Well, I have to go and get some rest because Joe really is looking forward to our marriage.

We Can't Afford to Love You Anymore

Grand was the happiest when he was opening a new present. He wasn't sure if it was the excitement of the unknown, or the surprise of guessing wrong, or just being able to show off his new gift to all his friends that made him so happy, but whatever it was, it made life worthwhile.

Grand's father managed to bring Grand a present every day when he got home from work. Sometimes his Dad got home very late, but he always woke Grand up to show him he hadn't forgotten. The days that Grand's father was out of town, Grand usually got his present via Federal Express.

By the time that Grand was six years old he had a basement so full of toys and other gifts that it became unusable for anything, except storage. Grand made tunnels through the piles and piles of items and even got lost one day in the maze he created. He escaped by pounding on the floor of the room above him until his mother heard him. She managed to follow the sound and found him nearly exhausted from all the pounding he had done. Together they were able to find their way out. After that experience Grand made marks on the floor so he could find his way back to the stairs from anywhere in his maze. It took some of the adventure out of his exploring, but his Mother had warned him if he ever got lost again she would donate all his toys to the Salvation Army.

Once Grand asked his parents how he got his name. The reason his father gave was that "That's Grand" is what he said when his wife told him they were going to have a baby. The reason his mother gave was that a "grand" is what it costs a week to buy gifts for him. "Very funny Mother," Grand laughed.

Then one day it happened. The worst thing Grand could ever imagine. No gift. No Federal Express delivery. No gift certificate. Not even an IOU. Grand wondered, "What gives?" Certainly not his father. At least not anymore.

Grand asked his mother if it was a National holiday and the Post Office was closed. She said it was not. He then asked if

Federal Express was on strike. They were not. Was his father sick? No. Was he broke? At this question Grand's mother started to cry. "What's wrong Mother?" Grand asked anxiously. "I'm sorry Honey," his mother stammered, "We can't afford to love you anymore." She then ran out of the room weeping uncontrollably, leaving Grand very alone and very worried.

After composing herself, Grand's mother came back into the room and tried to explain the situation. "Grand," she said almost in a whisper, "I didn't really mean we can't afford financially to love you; and we could never stop loving you emotionally for as long as we live. What I meant was that your Dad and I just can't afford, for your sake, to buy you toys every day any longer."

"That's okay," Grand replied, "Once every other day will be okay." "No, it won't," his Mother quietly answered. "Once a week?" Grand quickly implored. "No. Not ever, ever again," his Mother firmly, but hesitantly said.

The look on Grand's face was more than his Mother could take. She turned around to leave the room again, but then quickly turned around again and grabbed Grand and hugged him like she never had before. Grand was caught off guard because his Mother never had hugged him like this before. Either had his Dad. The only way he ever knew for certain that they did love him was by their buying him whatever he wanted, whenever he wanted it. By getting a gift every day of his life, Grand knew he was loved. At least he thought he knew he was loved. The notes on the cards that accompanied the gift always were signed "Love, Mom and Dad." Why would they say it if they didn't mean it? Why would they stop giving him gifts though?

"Mom," Grand tried to say through his Mother's sweater that was firmly against his mouth, "Why?"

It was a long story, but Grand's Mom knew it had to be told in its entirety or not at all. "Well, Grand," she started. "Your Father and I decided we do not want a son who only lives for the present. I mean that both literally and figuratively. You only seem to live for one day at a time and if you do look forward at all into the future, it is only to the next day and the next present."

104

Grand looked confused. He looked down at his feet. He looked up at the ceiling. He even looked deep inside his pockets. After not being able to find the answer anywhere, he looked into his Mother's eyes; and there he thought he saw an answer.

Mom's eyes were deep and dark and wet; and they reflected everything around her. In the center of her eyes was the reflection of Grand. Whenever Grand had looked into his own eyes in his reflection in his mirror all he ever saw was himself; never another person. Grand knew the images in his Mother's eyes were usually just light being bounced off her eyes too, but somehow he felt that this image was coming from somewhere deep within her.

"Mom," Grant implored, "What do you see when you look at me?" His Mom sighed deeply and proceeded to let Grand know everything she possibly could about him. At the same time though, she found herself telling Grand a lot about herself....

"Grand," she started. "When I look at you I see the most precious thing I have in this world. But I also see that you care only about yourself and your happiness. You never notice that your Father and I are only happy when you are happy. That's one reason we continued for all of these years to give you gifts...it made us happy. Maybe that makes us selfish too. Up till now is has felt right, but it doesn't anymore." Grand hesitantly agreed by nodding his head ever so slightly.

Every now and then Grand's Mom looked like she was going to cry again, but she managed to continue on with her explanation. "Your Father and I want you to be a success in life. For the longest time we thought that being a success meant that you would have everything you ever wanted, just like we do."

"What's wrong with that?", Grant asked. "It always has made me happy to have everything I want."

"Yes, I know," his Mom continued, "But you have never, ever managed to purposely make anyone else's life happy. Not even your Father's and mine. We have always been happy just because you were happy, but you never intentionally made an effort to try and make us happy. We just vicariously shared in your enjoyment. We pretended we were the ones getting the presents. We pretended we were the most important person in the world. We felt the way we wanted you to feel."

"But just the other day your Dad and I realized you were only happy because you were getting something every day of your life. We realized too, that we have never given you the opportunity to experience the happiness that giving to someone else can give to you. So starting tomorrow all the gifts that you have accumulated over the last six years are going to be donated by you to the Salvation Army and other needy charities; one gift each day until they are all gone."

"What?" Grand yelled. "That's not fair!"

"Quiet!", his Mother responded. "You can talk when I am finished." Grand sulked, but obediently became very quiet and very still. As Grand's eyes started filling with tears, his Mom continued to explain.

"You get to choose which gift goes each day. You get to decide which one goes first and which one goes last and the order of all the other ones in between. You will have plenty of time to enjoy the toys and games and other gifts that you feel are important to you now. Hopefully, though, long before your last present has been given away, you will find that you enjoy giving away the gifts much more than you ever did receiving them." "We'll even make a special effort to see where the gift you donate ends up. You will see that it will go to someone who really needs it; at least someone who needs it more than you do."

The next few minutes the room was silent, except for the sounds of deep breathing and heavy sighs. Grand and his Mom just looked at each other. Grand's Mom trying to communicate her innermost feelings through her eyes, while Grand was having no trouble at all showing bewilderment in his eyes.

Grand was both confused and stunned at the same time. What could he possibly say that would change things? What could he possibly do to make things right? What words were there that would undo all the years of his parents thinking that he had cared only about himself? There weren't any, but he knew he had to do what his Mom and Dad wanted. He knew the reason he loved his parents had nothing to do with them giving him presents each day. It hadn't hurt their relationship, but it would not have changed a bit how he felt about them if they had never given him anything but love. He wanted them to know it too.

He wanted to say "I love you, Mom." He wanted to say he didn't want any more toys, if that was what would make his parents happy. He wanted to say all these things and more, but the words kept getting stuck somewhere between his brain and his mouth.

Grand felt so bad for himself because he couldn't express his feelings to his Mom, and so sorry for his Mom, who thought that he didn't love her, that he started to cry harder than he ever had before. This time though, he was crying for someone else besides himself. This time the tears were real. This time he couldn't just turn the tears off by himself. His Mom pulled him into her arms and hugged him until Grand stopped sobbing. It took awhile, but Grand's Mom had all the time in the world for him now. That's all either she or Grand's Dad were going to give Grand anymore— their time. Grand did not realize it at the moment, but he would often look back on this day as the day he became rich. What, after all, could his parents have possibly given him that was more valuable than their time.